Canada's
Parliament Buildings

Canada's Parliament Buildings

Mark Bourrie

Hounslow Press
Toronto • Oxford

Canada's Parliament Buildings

Hounslow Press
A member of the Dundurn Group

Publisher: Anthony Hawke
Editor: Liedewy Hawke
Designer: Sebastian Vasile
Printer: Webcom
Front Cover Photograph: Andy Shott

Canadian Cataloguing in Publication Data

Bourrie, Mark, 1957-
    Canada's Parliament Buildings

ISBN 0-88882-190-5

1. Parliament Buildings (Ottawa, Ont.) - History.
I. Title.

NA4415. C220726 1996   725'.11'0971384   C96-930601-6

Publication was assisted by the **Canada Council**, the **Book Publishing Industry Development Program** of the **Department of Canadian Heritage**, and the **Ontario Arts Council**.

Care has been taken to trace the ownership of copyright material used in this book. The author and the publisher welcome any information enabling them to rectify any references or credit in subsequent editions.

Printed and bound in Canada.

Printed on recycled paper.

Hounslow Press	Hounslow Press	Hounslow Press
2181 Queen Street East	73 Lime Walk	250 Sonwil Drive
Suite 301	Headington, Oxford	Buffalo, NY
Toronto, Ontario, Canada	England	U.S.A. 14225
M4E 1E5	OX3 7AD	

CONTENTS

Acknowledgements

he author is indebted to many people of the Parliament Hill community: Heather Bradley, Andy Shott, and Audrey Dube of the Office of the Speaker of the House of Commons; House of Commons Speaker Gilbert Parent, who explained to me the importance of the parliamentary mace and its history; the staff of the House of Commons tour guide program, who rarely knew when I would attach myself to one of their trips through the buildings; Jean-Marc Cariffe of the Prime Minister's Office; the National Archives of Canada and the National Library of Canada; the staff of the Canadian Parliamentary Press Gallery, with a special thanks to Nelson Laframboise, Terry Guillon, and Joyce Kingston-Viens; Arthur Milnes, a treasure house of Canadian political lore; Rosaleen Dickson of the Hill Times, who provided interesting information about the Great Fire of 1916.

There is no way that this book could have been completed without the help of the generous and kind staff of the Library of Parliament; my editor, Liedewy Hawke; my publisher and friend, Tony Hawke, and, above all, my wife Marion, who keeps it all together.

Introduction

The voice of the people is said to be as the voice of God.

House of Commons,
Petition to King James I, 1604

The idea that the voice of the people holds wisdom, or should even be listened to, is not new. In small places, where people know one another and can judge for themselves the wisdom in the words of their neighbours, democracy is a system that arises fairly naturally. Nomadic groups, such as the aboriginal hunters of the Canadian subarctic and plains, have to be limited in size since hunting is an unpredictable and rather tricky way of making a living. Most hunting bands are made up of only a family or two, acting the way any family would. Ideas are shared, disagreements are worked out through argument, promises are made. If people aren't satisfied with the way things are going, they may simply leave the group. Anyone holding responsibility does so with the direct consent of the governed, and, if the people don't like the way things are run, the leader works out the problem with the unhappy followers, steps aside, or watches as his former friends pack up and go.

People who live on farms have a more stable food supply. If there is a surplus, populations rise. Towns and cities can be created. As a society becomes more complex, its members no longer know everyone in their region. Class systems arise, people compete for control of commerce and territory, citizens expect protection, and armies are created to protect the society from foreign invasion.

Most early states were simply tyrannies, developed to force people to do the bidding of a few leaders. The voice of the people can never be kept silent for very long, however. In time, the will of the people, their demand to be heard, has crumbled all of the great police states. Pharaohs, Greek city state tyrants, Caesars, absolute monarchs, Jacobins, all once terrified their citizens. Now they're gone, most often remembered only as part of high school history exams. Nazis, Communists, Peronists, Fascists, too, are fading, or have already left history's stage. Yet our one-thousand-year-old parliamentary system survives, flourishes, and is copied and adapted in most places that have embraced democracy.

Canada's parliamentary system has roots that go back far into the history of Europe and North America. We think of Canada as a new country, but it is one of the world's oldest parliamentary democracies. Some of the democratic ideas that are embedded in our political system took shape here before Europeans began colonizing North America.

Canada is the largest area ever to be governed by a truly democratic government. Our constitution envisions Canada as a federal state, meaning that power is shared between provincial governments, each representing the interests of a separate region, and a central government, which is expected to govern for the benefit of Canada as a whole.

The Parliament of Canada is a complex institution that uses written law, as well as the unwritten traditions of the British system, to determine how it is to function. Parliament is not just the House of Commons. It embraces the queen, represented in Canada by the governor general, along with the Senate, and the House of Commons. In theory, at least, the three branches of Parliament balance each other. Members of the ministry, who are the executive of the government, may be members of either the elected House of Commons or the appointed Senate. Ministers are selected by the prime minister, who also chooses the departments for which they will be responsible, but the prime minister must inform and consult the governor general, in the name of the queen. The governor general appoints the prime minister's choices, and, traditionally, new ministers are sworn in at Rideau Hall, the governor general's residence.

The buildings on Parliament Hill were built to be the physical centrepiece of this system. Their Gothic architecture is a reminder of the long history of the institution of Parliament. Inside, the political currents of our society are reflected by the ebb and flow of governments. Dramatic, colourful, brilliant, and, quite often, eccentric people, created these buildings and governed from them.

There is a sacredness within the walls of the old Gothic buildings. They are legislatures, offices, and meeting rooms. They are also shrines to our freedom. If anyone in the country really wants to feel like a Canadian, this little group of stone buildings is the place to visit. Good and bad governments come and go, but the hard-won right of the people to have their voice echo in the halls of Parliament endures, as it has down through the centuries.

Part One
Victoria's Choice

It seems like an act of insanity to have fixed the capital of this great country away from the civilization, intelligence and commercial enterprise of the Province, in a place that can never be a place of any importance. My confident belief is, notwithstanding the vast expense incurred here in public buildings, Ottawa will not be the capital four years hence.
Lord Monck, first governor general
of Canada, 1866

ord Monck was obviously not blessed with psychic powers or political foresight. Long after his prophecy, along with his name, was forgotten by Canadians, the Parliament Buildings still stand on a limestone outcrop bounded by the Ottawa River and the Rideau Canal.

Many Canadians feel a surge of patriotism when they come to Parliament Hill. There is no greater symbol of Canada than these great Gothic buildings. The Canadian flag seems to fly more proudly at the top of the Peace Tower than it does at any other place in the country.

Like the rest of Canada, Parliament Hill has its faults. In fact, it's geological faulting that created the hill in the first place. The Ottawa Valley is a limestone plain that, as a result of shifts in the earth's crust plates and innumerable earthquakes, has dropped more than four hundred metres since the time of the dinosaurs. The rocks of Parliament Hill were already ancient when those huge animals were alive. They were laid down 450 million years ago, during the Ordovician Period, when fish just started to evolve. The rocks of Parliament Hill are rich in fossils, and collectors have found rare specimens along the river's shore and behind the Supreme Court.

Unfortunately, the hill is not as solid as it looks. Millions of years ago, the Ottawa Valley and the Montreal region passed over a volcanic hot spot. Mount Royal and the hills south of Montreal are the remains of old volcanoes that pushed through the crust. Ottawa didn't erupt, but massive cracks caused the geology of the region to become a jumble of fractured cliffs. Later, during the ice ages, the land was pressed so low that the sea flooded the Ottawa Valley after the glaciers retreated. Nodules found in local streams contain eight-thousand-year-old fossil fish, frogs, and mammals. The bones of whales and seals often turn up in the region's gravel pits.

The land is still rebounding, causing small tremors that shake Parliament Hill. Geology may not be interesting to some Canadians, but it costs us all, since we've built our capital on a place that literally shakes and rolls. Much of the money that's spent on renovations and repairs on Parliament Hill goes towards repairing cracks in the stonework caused by those minor tremors.

The river below the hill, the Ottawa River, used to be eastern Canada's main highway. It was used for at least five thousand years by native travellers, who have left many traces of their camps on the Quebec side of its waters. The Ottawa River was the main link between the St. Lawrence

Valley and the Great Lakes. Colonisers followed the native trade routes. Think of any explorer: Champlain, Brûlé, Radisson, LaVérendrye, MacKenzie, or Thompson, along with the fur traders of the Northwest Company — they all used this river. Four hundred years ago, it was a tortuous water highway, laced with strong currents, broken by rapids and fierce waterfalls, blocked by powerful native bands who demanded a toll from travellers. Bordered by poison ivy,it was a breeding ground for half a dozen kinds of biting flies. In their journals, few explorers and missionaries had good things to say about the Ottawa River canoe route.

By the end of the War of 1812, some permanent clearings were appearing in the woods around Parliament Hill. United Empire Loyalists fleeing the American Revolution had settled across the river in Hull. Loggers had begun surveying the abundant white pine and oak timber of the valley, which was needed in Britain to build ships for the Royal Navy. After the War of 1812, people living in Upper and Lower Canada began wondering if they could use the Ottawa River to bypass the upper St. Lawrence River, which could so easily be controlled by U.S. forces. There was no natural water route between Lake Ontario and the Ottawa River, but construction of a canal was possible by using the waters of the Rideau River and its tributary lakes. Beginning in 1816, surveyors combed the wilderness, looking for the best route between Lake Ontario and the Ottawa River. Ten years later, they found it.

By then, a canal wasn't really needed for strategic reasons, and it wasn't a project that could make money from commercial shipping. But that's hindsight. Within twenty years, railways would begin linking the towns of Canada. Canals would be a drain on the public purse for more than a century, until the boom in pleasure boating finally made them financially sound.

Col. John By, an engineer and a man of some vision, realized that the northern terminal of the Rideau Canal, which he chose near the mouth of the Rideau River, was a place of great natural beauty, rich farmland, and valuable timber. It was far enough inland to be relatively safe from a U.S. invasion. He went out on a bit of a limb and predicted the city would one day be a capital. Then he backed his theory with his own money by buying a large parcel of land just south of what is now downtown Ottawa. He suggested to his friends that they do likewise, and the shrewd ones followed his advice. At first glance, the investments were risky. Before By built the Rideau Canal, most of today's downtown Ottawa was a beaver swamp which drained into the Ottawa River at the site where By built the canal's last locks.

After the canal was built, the earl of Dalhousie, the British colony's governor, spent 750 pounds to buy what is now Parliament Hill from its former owner, who had purchased the property after the War of 1812 for a miserly twelve pounds. Lord Dalhousie had planned to build a fort on the site to protect the canal. Only a set of wooden barracks was built, while a rough little logging town sprang up on the far side of the canal, which is now the Byward Market and Lower Town. The Rideau and Chaudière falls were tamed for mills, and great rafts of timber began floating toward Quebec City.

The first settlers were infamous for their drinking and the nasty fights that broke out in the streets in front of the town's many taverns. Sometimes riots developed that could only be quelled by mustering the troops from the garrison that guarded the canal, and by calling out the local militia.

By mid-century, however, the old barracks on the hill were deserted. The retired sergeant who kept the gardens around them was gone, and the site was used for the town's fall agricultural show. Strategically, time seemed to have passed it by.

No one, in the first half of the nineteenth century, would have made a large bet that the disorderly little logging town named Bytown after Colonel By would ever amount to much. In the early years of Queen Victoria's reign, only a handful of people considered it possible that the town might become the nation's capital. True, the colony's capital always seemed to be on the move, but it found homes in cities which were much more refined than the hamlet at the mouth of the Rideau Canal.

During the French regime, Quebec City served as the capital of France's colonies on the North American mainland, and it kept the status of capital after the surrender of the colony to Britain in 1763. The British expected the city to remain the seat of government. Construction on fortifications and public buildings continued for several decades, but, at the same time, politicians in London were concerned with political issues arising from the American Revolution. Many English-speaking people were moving into the Great Lakes region, far from Quebec City. They demanded a voice in government. In 1791, the British Parliament passed a bill that split Quebec into Upper and Lower Canada in order to give a measure of political autonomy to the United Empire Loyalists who had left the former thirteen colonies to live under British rule.

Lower Canada's capital continued to be Quebec City. Upper Canada's first capital was Niagara-on-the-Lake. The first Parliament of Upper Canada met there on November 17, 1792. Its members included representatives from Detroit and other parts of the then-northwestern United States that were still occupied by Britain. Niagara-on-the-Lake was unsatisfactory for several reasons: it was too close to the United States, the village was small and difficult to reach by land, and most new settlers were passing it by to build homesteads in southwestern and central Ontario. The provincial capital was transferred to York (Toronto), where it remained until 1840, when the British government decided to re-unite the provinces of Upper and Lower Canada in the wake of the Rebellions of 1837.

Between 1841 and 1867, the Province of Canada was served by a wandering Parliament. This transience was due to a number of factors, most of which reflected badly on the cities involved, on their citizens, and on the politicians who were members of the colonial legislature. At first, Kingston, Montreal, Quebec City, and Toronto took turns serving as the capital, but by 1859, when the foundations were laid for the buildings on Parliament Hill, Ottawa had won out.

Kingston had proven to be too primitive for the politicians, who complained constantly that it was inaccessible and boring. The city, then and now, is one of the most beautiful in Canada. It was central to the united colony and was expected to serve as a bastion of Anglican conservatism. Several handsome buildings still stand in Kingston from its days as capital. Parliament met in the city's hospital.

Montreal, the next stop on the colonial Parliament's journey, proved to be an unfortunate choice. In 1848, a mob, outraged at the signing of the Rebellion Losses Bill, burned the Parliament building and its twenty-thousand-volume library.

From 1849 until 1865, the functions of the capital of the Province of Canada were moved back and forth between Toronto and Quebec City while leaders of all of the country's major cities argued over the location of a permanent capital. Moving the legislature was a very unsatisfactory arrangement, since, each time Parliament

In 1848, a Montreal mob rioted and burned the legislative building of the Province of Canada. The parliament moved from city to city until Ottawa was chosen to be the permanent capital.

(National Archives of Canada C 2726)

changed place, its records, library, and furniture had to be crated and shipped. Politicians and civil servants had to find new homes or rooming houses, and there was little sense of political continuity. Until politicians could agree on the site of a permanent capital, this strange arrangement continued.

In 1857, the question of the location of Canada's capital was referred to Queen Victoria. Everyone knew that the city that was chosen would enjoy a financial windfall, so the largest communities in Canada vied for the honour. Kingston, Montreal, Quebec City, and Toronto were in the running. Sir Edmund and Lady Head, friends of Queen Victoria's, had visited Bytown, however, and lobbied for that town. The queen agreed, leaving the politicians to fight over the matter. The queen's choice wasn't accepted gracefully.

One government fell over the issue, and, while the queen herself was above criticism, the city that she chose was not.

Once the dust had settled, Queen Victoria's preference was respected. The government set aside $480,000 for the construction of a legislative building and two departmental structures that were expected to house nearly all the employees of the government of Canada. Four kilometres away, government agents negotiated a lease for Rideau Hall, a Georgian villa built in the wilderness on the east side of the Rideau River. It was supposed be the temporary home of the governor general, until a better mansion could be built across the canal from the Parliament Buildings, in what is now Major's Hill Park. Soon after Confederation, however, the government purchased Rideau Hall and began expanding it to a suitably vice-regal size.

Most of the country's best architects submitted proposals for the important new buildings. We are used to the magnificent Gothic structures that were eventually built, but if other bids had been successful, we might have had a Parliament Building that looked like an Elizabethan mansion, a classical Greek temple, or a Norman castle. Those were some of the styles that were turned down.

A Gothic revival was under way in North America and Britain during the middle years of the nineteenth century. The new British Parliament Building, built to replace the ancient Westminster Palace which burned in the 1830s, was constructed in a high Gothic style.

Gothic designs were seldom seen in North America. Architects of public buildings in the United States always used classical designs of pillars, round domes, and clean lines.

Most of Canada's public buildings constructed before 1860, including the Kingston Parliament building and Cobourg's Victoria Hall, were designed in the classical style, reviving Greek and Roman columns, domes, and great exterior stairways. In the mid-1800s, that style fell by the wayside in Canada, except in the great railway stations built in Canada's larger cities.

The Gothic revival was to give Canada the Parliament Buildings, Toronto's University College and Old City Hall, and a host of new churches and cathedrals that appeared throughout Canada in the latter years of the century.

In retrospect, the Gothic style was probably the best choice for the Ottawa Parliament Buildings. When seen from across the canal or from the river banks, the picturesque building site, with its soaring cliffs, is highlighted by these edifices which seem to reach skyward with their towers, chimneys, and iron work. With the exception of Athens' Acropolis and Scotland's Edinburgh Castle, no national capital has such a dramatic landscape.

THE NEW CAPITAL

LIKE MOST COMPLEX enterprises, the construction of the Parliament Buildings soon ran into trouble. The hill itself, with its soft clay soil and uneven bedrock, was an expensive nuisance. The trouble started there and increased as the buildings took shape.

Thomas McGreevy of Quebec City won the contest for the original Centre Block, settling on a sum of $348,500 for its construction. Jones, Haycock and Clarke of Port Hope, Ontario, won the competition for the two departmental buildings, which are now called the East and West Blocks. Their bid was for $278,810.

The young Prince of Wales (later Edward VII) laid the cornerstone for the Centre Block on September 1, 1860. He was visiting the frontier city to look over the new capital

Inflation, poor planning, a shortage of workers, and engineering problems caused the construction of the Parliament Buildings to become a national scandal. Construction workers are laying pipe while stonemasons work on the facade of the original Centre Block.

(National Archives of Canada C 38764)

A jumble of rocks, a half-finished building, and no one around but a boy on a fence: for several years, politicians and taxpayers worried that the construction project would never be finished.

(National Archives of Canada C 3040)

site, ride the log rafts down the slide at the Chaudière Falls, and enjoy as much of the city's social life as he could.

The cost estimates set by the builders and the government were very precise, but, at the same time, unrealistic. Basic necessities such as heating ducts were left out of the plans. No money had been put aside to cover the cost of channelling through the limestone to lay down plumbing pipes. Before long, the entire project had become a scandal. The seventeen hundred workers, who often weren't paid on time, walked off the job. Politicians and government officials blamed the contractors for the escalating costs. The contractors felt that the civil servants were making unrealistic demands. Eventually, after an inquiry that caused a complete shutdown of work on the

Much of the stone that was used for the Parliament Buildings was quarried locally. Masons cut blocks of Nepean sandstone on the construction site and used it to build the exteriors of the three departmental buildings.

(National Archives of Canada C 18355)

half-finished buildings, the government took over the project. When construction was finally finished, it had cost ten times more than the government had expected to pay.

Originally, the little city on the hill was supposed to be the capital of the united provinces of Canada East and Canada West. The United States Civil War, which had caused some of the inflation that pushed up the building costs, was also a spur to the British colonies to consider a wider union. By 1865, when the war ended, provincial politicians were

As delegates to the Quebec and Charlottetown conferences put together a new country, the Centre Block rose from amid a shanty town of temporary construction huts on Parliament Hill. The crane is perched on the Victoria Tower. Its clock would be installed later.

(National Archives of Canada C 3039)

close to agreement on the constitution of the new Dominion. In the fall of that year, they moved into their new offices while workers were completing the project. On 1 July 1867, Confederation was a reality, and the three new buildings, which towered over the lumber mill town of eighteen thousand people, were ready for the new government.

Today's visitors to Parliament Hill are often amazed that the three original buildings could house nearly all of the

The East Block, half-finished and partly hidden by scaffolding, became the headquarters of the governor general and the prime minister after Confederation. The large wooden scaffold on the right was used by masons to build the southwest tower.

(National Archives of Canada C 09978)

Confederation-era employees of the federal government. The civil service did fit quite comfortably into the new complex. The original legislative building, the Centre Block, was much smaller and less efficient in its use of space than the present building, and the East Block was also somewhat smaller than the pretty little Gothic structure that we see today.

Massive vaults that held the country's foreign cash and gold reserves had been built in the basement of the East

As the first members of Canada's new Parliament made their way to Ottawa, the finishing touches were still being added to the buildings on Parliament Hill. At the time of Confederation, an ornate dome for the top of the main tower of the Centre Block was still on the drawing board.

(National Archives of Canada C 21954)

Block, along with offices for the governor general, the prime minister, the Cabinet, and the civil servants who helped run the departments.

The House of Commons chamber, built for the pre-Confederation legislature of the united Canadas, had to be renovated to hold sixty-four new chairs and thirty-two new desks, belonging to the members of Parliament from New Brunswick and Nova Scotia. Even the press gallery had to be rebuilt and expanded to hold twenty-two reporters, instead of twelve.

When the new Dominion Parliament held its first session in 1867, the complex of buildings was ready, except for the library. For nine more years, Canada's official records

The original Senate chamber, with its ornate throne and leather chairs, was still a very plain room when this picture was taken at the time of Confederation. The modern Senate follows the floor plan of the 1867 chamber.

(National Archives of Canada PA 8342)

and the reference books relied on by politicians and the officers of Parliament remained in boxes or in stacks on the floor of a room in the Centre Block.

Since its construction, the Centre Block has burned and been rebuilt. Craftspeople have added to the rich stone carvings of all the Parliament Buildings. For example, on the East Block, students of heraldry can easily find the governor general's entrance by looking for the royal coat of arms, while symbols over another door show sheaves of wheat, to remind visitors that the building was home to the Department of Agriculture. Wrought iron work, which few

The original Cabinet room in the East Block was dominated by a map of Canada. Ministers each had a drawer in the round table, and the clerk of the Privy Council had a desk at the side of the room.

(National Archives of Canada PA 8388)

tourists and Parliament Hill veterans stop to examine, was recognized in its day as being among the best on the continent. The big iron gates that once protected the main entrance to the Hill were considered such marvels that they were taken to the United States to be exhibited at trade shows and a World's Fair. Parliament Hill is a showcase of the work of hundreds of artists and craftspeople, a record in stone of Canada's past, along with the nation's hopes and aspirations.

A visitor to the newly finished Canadian capital would have seen a Parliament Hill that resembled the one that

The original prime minister's office in the East Block was not very fancy: a leather chair, a bearskin rug and a desk. The building was cold. One washroom was reserved for the governor general. Everyone else, including the prime minister, had to share the second one.
(National Archives of Canada PA 8650).

After Confederation, extra seats had to be added to the legislature of the Province of Canada to make room for members of Parliament from New Brunswick and Nova Scotia. This is a view of the original House of Commons from the government side.
(National Archives of Canada PA 8361)

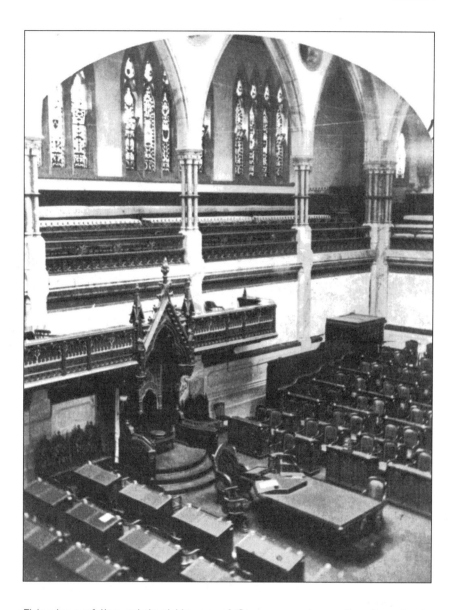

This view of the original House of Commons shows the Speaker's chair and the clerks' table. The press gallery is the small balcony directly above the Speaker's chair.

(National Archives of Canada C 3874)

Before the completion of the Library of Parliament in 1876, records and books were stored in attic rooms in the Centre Block.

(National Archives of Canada PA 12487)

In the summer of 1875, builders posed on top of the wooden frame of the dome of the new Library of Parliament. The library is one of Canada's finest examples of Gothic revival architecture.
(National Archives of Canada C 80781)

With the completion of the dome on the Victoria Tower and the construction of the Library of Parliament, Canada had one of the world's most beautiful legislative buildings.
(National Archives of Canada C 15106)

The Library of Parliament dome originally had a slate roof. Linking the library to the rest of the Centre Block was the reading room where the Great Fire of 1916 began.

(National Archives of Canada PA 138522)

exists today, but there are important differences. In size, the present complex is larger than that of 1867. There are now more buildings. The Confederation Building is the newest of the Gothic structures on Parliament Hill. It was built in 1927 to house members of Parliament and government officials. Across Wellington Street are edifices that house the Prime Minister's Office and the Privy Council Office, as well as buildings containing offices for the Senate and House of Commons, and a media building.

    The three main buildings on Parliament Hill occupy a roughly square piece of land that measures about 350 metres on each side. The hill itself is about sixty metres high, the highest point along the Ottawa River in this vicinity.

Looking uphill, from left to right, a visitor sees structures and architecture that didn't exist at Confederation. The West Block's magnificent Mackenzie Tower was built about a decade after Canada was founded. The roof of that building, along with those of the other two blocks, was made of multicoloured Vermont slate, instead of the copper sheeting you see today. The Parliament Buildings' copper roofs date from this century.

Except for the rearrangement of furniture and the addition of sophisticated computer equipment, the interior of the Library of Parliament is virtually unchanged since this picture was taken in 1876.

The original Centre Block, the edifice that comes to people's minds when they think of Parliament Hill, vaguely resembled the building that visitors see today. The old structure was smaller and one storey lower than the modern one. Its clock tower was much less impressive than the Peace Tower. The original tower was about the same height as the Mackenzie Tower on the West Block.

From the front, the East Block looks about the same as it did at the time of Confederation. A later expansion added a wing to the rear of the building.

The most noticeable change on Parliament Hill since Confederation may well be the improvement in landscaping. The builders cut down every mature tree on the hill, along with the ancient small cedars that clung to the cliffs. Only newly planted saplings provided shade. The lawn was unsightly. Originally, a fountain and walkways were to have been built on it. Instead, rough paths linked the buildings. The outlines of them can still be seen from tall buildings nearby, despite years of fertilizing and re-sodding. It makes sense that, after such huge construction cost overruns, there was no money left for landscaping.

Across the street, the brown sandstone Langevin Block, modern setting of the Prime Minister's Office, didn't exist in 1867, nor did most of the buildings downtown. Sparks Street was a row of stores and boarding houses. In front of one of them, D'Arcy McGee, a Father of Confederation, was assassinated. Others were home to politicians, Cabinet ministers, civil servants, itinerant members of the press gallery, and the officials who try to make Parliament run smoothly.

Work progressed slowly on the capital's buildings as the new Dominion expanded. By World War I, Ottawa had become a fairly comfortable, vibrant city. Then, mid-way through the war, disaster struck Parliament Hill.

Part Two
The Great Fire

O n the morning of February 3, 1916, Edgar Rhodes was chosen to be Deputy Speaker of the House of Commons. The job was an honour that carried with it some responsibilities. Among them was the task of presiding over night sittings, giving the Speaker time to entertain in his private quarters.

Later on that day, in the bitter cold and gathering darkness, members of Parliament, a few senators, and some members of the press gallery made their way into the Centre Block for the evening sitting. Even though World War I was raging, that evening's debate was supposed to be routine: a fisheries bill.

Down the hall from the House of Commons, MP Francis Glass was reading a newspaper in the Commons Reading Room, just outside the doors of the library. Not far away was Mme Verville, the wife of the member of Parliament for Maisonneuve. Newspapers from across Canada, along with thousands of records going back to the French regime, were crowded into the small room. Somehow, some of those papers began to burn. Within a few seconds Mme Verville saw smoke, then flames. She ran from the room.

Glass called for a constable. They tried to put out the fire, but the pine interior of the room was heavily varnished and glistened with oil. Burning papers flew around. The first Centre Block, a warren of small rooms with wooden walls, heavy varnish, and oiled woodwork, was doomed.

Phone lines connected the Centre Block with a fire hall nearby. The alarm sounded at 8:57 and firefighters were on the Hill three minutes later. Near the Reading Room was the entrance to the Library of Parliament. One of the librarians, Connolly McCormac, with the help of a Commons messenger, raced to the steel doors and closed them before the flames could spread to the white pine interior of the library. It was an act of remarkable foresight.

Deputy Speaker Rhodes was enjoying his first and only time presiding over the House of Commons in its original home. Three MPs, Glass among them, along with Commons staff, rushed into the chamber to sound the alarm to the twenty members who were involved in the fisheries bill debate.

"There's a big fire in the reading room. Get out quickly," Glass shouted to the surprised MPs, the handful of people in the press gallery, and the spectators lining the edge of the visitor's gallery.

Rhodes led the members as they quickly rose and prepared to leave the chamber. While they gathered up their papers, a huge flame penetrated a wall of the House of Commons. For reasons that have never been explained, none of the MPs nor members of the Commons staff took the golden mace from its table in front of the Deputy Speaker.

The press gallery reporters and people in the visitors gallery escaped without serious injury.

The fire, made a roar as it spread through the wooden corridors of the Centre Block. The MPs had barely left the

House of Commons before the fire spread to the ornate wooden interior. The twenty MPs, nearly lost in the smoke-filled halls, held hands as they tried to escape from the building. Prime Minister Robert Borden had watched the fisheries debate for a while, then retired to his office to deal with some correspondence. He was warned by a Commons messenger that the building was on fire. The prime minister and the messenger crawled on their hands and knees in order to stay below the smoke and found their way to a stairway. Borden emerged outside the building without a hat or a coat and was given help by people in the crowd that was already starting to form around the burning building. A member of his staff went to the prime minister's home to fetch winter clothes and boots.

Fire broke out in the Centre Block on the night of 3 February 1916, destroying the country's premiere landmark. In this photo, taken about five hours after the fire started, the Victoria Tower is silhouetted by the flames.

(National Archives of Canada C 10079)

By then, people were fleeing the building from windows. A rather amazing number of MPs were working in their offices or entertaining guests inside the building on the night of the fire. Michel Delisle was getting a haircut in the barber shop in the basement when flames shot through the ceiling. Delisle told the nervous barber, "There's no need to hurry. Give me a close shave." The barber was more sensible, and Delisle's session ended rather hurriedly.

Delisle was not the only parliamentarian to have a close shave that night. Two MPs made a rope from towels and climbed down the outside of the edifice. MP Martin Burrell barely escaped. Seeing no way to get out of his office unscathed, he ran through a wall of fire and into the arms of a couple of his colleagues. Burrell was given first aid by two members who were medical doctors, then taken to hospital, where he was treated for serious burns.

Seven people died in the fire. Many more would have been lost, if not for the skill and courage of the firefighters, police, and soldiers, who worked through the night.

Mme H.A. Bray and Mme Louis Morin, who had been staying with the wife of House of Commons Speaker Albert Sévigny in the Speaker's apartment, were taking part in a piano recital when Sévigny rushed in to say the building was on fire. The Speaker made sure everyone, including the two young Sévigny children, got out of the apartment, but Mme Morin and Mme Bray went back to get their fur coats. The Speaker, after leaving his children with a constable, tried to re-enter the apartment in order to rescue his two guests but was driven back by heat and smoke. Firefighters tried to rescue the women by entering the apartment through ladders from the outside of the building. One firefighter was overcome by smoke, but a second man found the two fire victims. They had died of smoke inhalation.

Three federal government employees were also killed. Jean Baptiste Laplante, assistant clerk of the House of Commons, was trapped in a second floor room and overcome by smoke. Randolph Fanning, a post office worker, along with Alphonse Desjardin, a steamfitter, had volunteered to help fight the fire. They joined a police officer whose name was also Alphonse Desjardin, and who was a nephew of the House of Commons employee. All three men died when a heavy stone ventilation tower behind the Senate crashed down on them.

Bowman Law, an MP who had left the House of Commons during the fishery debate, died in his office on the top floor of the Parliament Building. Law, who had served in the House of Commons for more than twenty years, was sadly mourned by his colleagues.

The city firefighters who arrived so promptly when the first alarm sounded realised they couldn't control the blaze or keep it from spreading to the East Block, which was threatened by wind-blown embers. They sent out a call to the other fire halls in the city and to the troops that were training at Lansdowne Park. Firefighters and soldiers arrived quickly. The troops kept the crowds back from the building and helped rescue art and furniture from the Senate side. Within an hour, calls went out to towns around Ottawa and to Montreal for extra firefighters. The mayor of Montreal, Médéric Martin, who was also a member of Parliament, placed a call to his city from the Château Laurier, requesting a special train to rush his city's best equipment to Ottawa. Before midnight, when it was obvious that the East and West Blocks were saved and there was nothing that could be done for the Centre Block, Martin withdrew his order.

Fire had spread to the library roof, but the city firefighters quickly extinguished it. For the rest of the night,

Firefighters had only small steam pumps to fight the fire, which gutted the interior of the Centre Block but left much of the stone facade standing.

(National Archives of Canada RD 243)

they kept their hoses trained on the library, knowing that the rest of the building was doomed.

At the height of the fire, when it was obvious that the building was lost, Prime Minister Borden held a meeting with his senior ministers in the Château Laurier. They decided to look for a temporary meeting place for Parliament and to order an investigation into the cause of the fire. Most people believed that the fire was an act of wartime sabotage. Governor General Arthur, duke of Connaught, who was a son of Queen Victoria, rushed to Parliament Hill from Rideau Hall when he heard about the fire. He was joined by Opposition Leader Sir Wilfrid Laurier, who had left a downtown concert.

In the ruins of the Victoria Tower, salvagers found the clock tower bell that had chimed the hours until it fell after midnight of 3 February 1916. It now has an honoured place behind the library.

(Photo: Mark Bourrie)

Soon after Laurier arrived on the Hill, the roof of the ornate building collapsed, sending a wave of sparks towards the East Block. By midnight, only three hours after the fire started, one last great drama was left to be played out: the collapse of the building's bell tower.

The Victoria Tower was directly in the path of the fire, and by eleven the flames had reached its ground floor. For the next hour, they burned towards the tower's clock. The great bell of the clock struck midnight before it came crashing down. It was later recovered from the ruins and is now on display on the Ottawa River lookout behind the Library of Parliament.

Because the fire had spread so swiftly, very little was saved from the House of Commons side of the building. The mace and all the other furnishings of the House of Commons were lost, along with thousands of records, office furniture, and portraits.

Because the fire reached the Senate side much later, the beautiful painting of Queen Victoria by John Partridge, which had also survived the Montreal Parliament fire, was saved by a police constable and A.H. Todd, a member of the Senate staff. His uncle Alpheus Todd, assistant librarian to the Legislative Assembly, had rescued the same picture in Montreal. Both men cut the painting from its heavy frame, and visitors to the Centre Block can see that it has been remounted on canvas. Two very valuable paintings, of King George III and his wife Queen Charlotte, believed to have been painted by Sir Joshua Reynolds, were also rescued, but portraits of Edward VII, Queen Alexandra, George V and Queen Mary, were lost. Copies now hang, along with the rescued pictures, in the lobby of the Senate. Some people believe the painting of Queen Victoria is placed near the front door to make its rescue easier.

A soldier guards the small pile of furniture saved from the Senate: a few roll-top desks, some chairs, and a few pictures.

(National Archives of Canada RD 244)

The morning after the fire, several more blazes broke out in the ruins of the building. Firefighters pour more water into the ruins of the reading room where the fire started. Three men were killed nearby when a stone wall fell.

(National Archives of Canada RD 244)

From the West Block, the ice-covered ruins of the building hid much of the interior damage caused by the fire. The surviving walls were expected to be used in the reconstruction but later proved to be unsafe.

(National Archives of Canada PA 9237)

The Senate mace was saved and was later loaned to the House of Commons until a new mace could be made in London by the goldsmiths' guild. Other furniture was heaped in a desolate pile in front of the statue of Sir John A. Macdonald, guarded all night by a soldier.

The rescued furniture and paintings were hardly enough to furnish a new Canadian Parliament, but at least there are a few surviving mementos from that first edifice.

Meanwhile, the country had to be governed.

The organization of the makeshift Parliament was remarkably swift. At 3 P.M. the day after the fire, members met in the rotunda of the Victoria Museum, while the

The House of Commons met in the Victoria Museum, now the Canadian Museum of Nature, until the Centre Block was rebuilt. Sir Wilfrid Laurier lay in state here when he died in 1920.

(National Archives of Canada PA 139684)

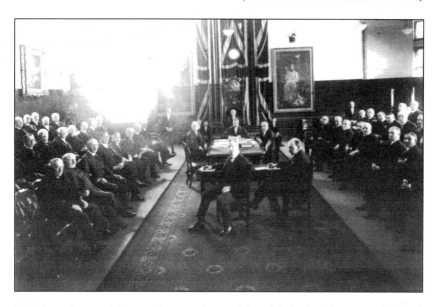

The Senate met in another gallery of the Victoria Museum. Behind the throne are pictures saved from the fire.

(National Archives of Canada C 22916)

Senate, with some irony, settled into its new quarters which was a room that had been a gallery for "fossils and leviathans." An investigation was already under way to determine if the fire had been set by enemy agents — a charge that was being made in huge headlines on the front pages of the country's newspapers. Visitors to the museum can see the place where, for four years, Canada's laws were made. It is the large, open space directly behind the huge wooden doors of the historic museum. A makeshift press gallery was installed on a sort of bridge between two staircases on the south side of the building, while visitors sat along balconies on the upper floors. The museum has

Once engineers determined that the ruins of the old Centre Block could not be used in the new building's construction, the old stone walls were torn down and the site was leveled for a new building.
(National Archives of Canada PA 130624)

changed very little since that time: rare footage of Sir Wilfrid Laurier's funeral shows the procession leaving a museum entrance that hasn't changed in eight decades.

That spring, the government received bad news about the ruins of the old Centre Block. The Borden administration had wanted to rebuild and restore the original building, perhaps expanding it by another storey, but the architects and contractors found that the ruins were not salvageable. The fire had destroyed the cement that held the blocks together, making the walls too weak to be of any value. Secrets about the old building were also being revealed. Because of the cost overruns back in the 1860s, contractors had given in to the temptation to cut corners. Some foundations could barely hold up the old building, let alone

By the summer of 1916, work had begun on the basement and foundations of the new Centre Block. Builders hurried to have the new Centre Block finished while Parliament met in the Victoria Museum.

(National Archives of Canada C 6321)

be of use for an expanded structure. The Borden government, therefore, decided to level the entire site, except, of course, for the library, and build a new structure that would fit in with the East and West Blocks. The library remained forlornly in place while the construction site was prepared. The little dome, sitting alone on Parliament Hill, was commemorated for many years on the back of the dollar bill.

The duke of Connaught re-laid the building's corner stone on 1 September 1916. Fifty-six years before, the same stone had been set in place by his brother Edward, Prince of Wales. Inside the stone, which can be seen in the northeast wall of the Centre Block, was placed a bundle containing five- and ten-dollar gold coins minted in 1912 (the first Canadian gold issue minted in Canada), a set of 1916-issue coins, postage stamps, and newspapers.

Three years after the disastrous fire, some of the offices in the new Centre Block were being used by members of Parliament and their staffs. Construction sheds still surround the unfinished building in this 1921 picture.

(National Archives of Canada PA 12925)

Builders add another stone to the walls of the Peace Tower as it rises above the West Block in the background.

(National Archives of Canada C 38750)

The Borden government expected the rebuilt Centre Block to be ready within a year of the cornerstone ceremony, but that turned out to be impossible. Wartime shortages, combined with the larger new design, caused problems for contractors. Even after the war was over, the construction of the new Centre Block was nearly as problem-ridden as the first construction project on the hill. By late 1919, however, offices were being moved into the Spartan new building. Early the next year, it was formally opened.

The cornerstone of the original Centre Block was salvaged from the ruins and built into the northeast wall of the new building.

(Photo: Mark Bourrie)

Part Three
The Contemporary Centre Block

The new building was quite different from the original Centre Block. For one thing, the present building is a storey higher, and is longer and wider. It is also less ornate, and built with more modern methods. For all its Gothic architectural flourishes and its ornate stonework, it is essentially a steel-framed, concrete, six-storey office building with a facing of sandstone. Its interior is virtually fireproof, with limestone walls and marble floors replacing the oiled and varnished wood of the original structure. The cost of the new structure was nearly $12 million.

The years have taken their toll on the building: its electrical system, heating machinery, and insulation have had to be replaced. Technological innovations such as computers and cable TV couldn't have been foreseen in the early 1920s, so adjustments have had to be made. Still, the Centre Block survived for seventy years without a major overhaul.

Most tourists see only the visitors' centre on the first floor, the Peace Tower and the ornate legislative chambers, the Memorial Chamber, the library and Hall of Honour. Due

Confederation Hall is one of the world's great modern Gothic
interiors. It is the foyer of the Centre Block.

(Photo: Andy Shott)

to security considerations, few visitors have access to the gorgeous hallways of the third floor, near the Prime Minister's Office. The rest of the building is generally utilitarian: hallways with stark stone walls and marble floors. Some doors on the office floors are carved with delightful flowers and small faces, but, with the exception of a few rooms, the more interesting sections of the building are open to the public.

Most visitors are struck by the artistry of the stonework in the Centre Block's great chambers and hallways. Carving began during the construction of the new building but stopped in the early years of the Great Depression. Cléophas Soucy was appointed chief carver in

Sculptor Eleanor Milne created many of the beautiful carvings in the Centre Block, including this work, which shows a teacher and children.

(Photo: Andy Shott)

Carvers' work graces many out-of-the-way places, like this corner in the Centre Block.

(Photo: Andy Shott)

1936. The great unicorn and lion that flank the entrance to the Centre Block were carved by Coeur de Lion McCarthy, Soucy's assistant. Two years after Soucy's appointment, all of the outside carving was completed. Inside, work continued, except during World War II. In 1962, Eleanor Milne was appointed national stone carver. She was largely

Leather chairs line the edge of Confederation hall, while, above, a stone gallery links the prime minister's office and the Cabinet room to the Senate side of the Centre Block.

(National Archives of Canada PA 22417)

responsible for the elaborate sculpture in the House of Commons foyer, on which she worked at night, after the House finished its business. Sculpting continues, making the Centre Block a dynamic memorial to Canada. There is space throughout the building for more commemorative art, just as there are more Canadians who, through service to the country, will deserve to be recorded in this most important of public buildings.

The most impressive work of these carvers was Confederation Hall, a masterpiece of stone masonry and sculpture. It is the lobby at the main entrance of the Centre Block. Eight outer columns support large, intricately carved fan vaults, which meet at the central column and its great fan vault. These arches symbolise how the central government and the provinces of Canada give support and strength to each other.

Neptune, representing the three oceans that border Canada, rests at the bottom of the central column. His presence reminds us of Canada's motto: "From Sea to Sea," and of the poetic lines that are carved over the Centre Block's front doors: "The wholesome sea is at her gates, Her gates both east and west." The floor is designed as a giant mariner's compass, with the wavy designs around its edge adding more ocean symbolism.

On the smaller columns are carved the coats of arms of the provinces and their capital cities, along with sculpture of native people, trappers, woodsmen, miners and sailors.

A hallway runs east-west through Confederation Hall. To the left, it leads to the foyer of the House of Commons; on the right, to the foyer of the Senate.

The hallway leading from Confederation Hall to the House of Commons passes a small committee room. Its doorway is adorned with carvings of killer whales. The portraits of prime ministers lines this hallway. As visitors approach the Commons foyer, the atmosphere becomes more charged, especially in the late afternoon of a typical Commons work day, when dozens of reporters and television technicians crowd the foyer and parts of the hall for "scrums" with politicians. The media scrum is a Canadian parliamentary institution. In the United States and Great Britain, the press doesn't have the same free access to politicians that Canadian media enjoy. After question period, Cabinet ministers seem to be swallowed up in a mass of people and microphones. The prime minister and opposition party leaders are usually interviewed from roped-off areas, although the prime minister will sometimes take questions from the stairway at the far west end of the Commons foyer. This flight of stairs leads up to the prime minister's office, on the third floor.

THE HOUSE OF COMMONS

IN SOME WAYS, the House of Commons has the look and feel of a church. Parliament has its roots in the medieval past, when English kings called their nobles together to raise taxes. These parliaments could meet anywhere. By the seventeenth century, however, the English House of Commons had a permanent home in St. Stephen's Chapel in the sprawling Westminster Palace. In the past, members of Parliament sat in a circle, on bags of wool or straw. At the end of the eighteenth century, members sat on benches lining the walls, in a sort of tiered bleachers structure. By the time of the Napoleonic Wars, the physical traditions of the House of Commons were in place: government and Opposition sitting two swords' lengths apart; a Speaker sitting on a raised chair, behind the clerk; members of the press looking on, recording the debates. The mace, a

During Question Period, the House of Commons becomes a battleground between the government and opposition parties. The Speaker, centre, chairs the debate and maintains decorum.

(Photo: Andy Shott)

symbol of power, signified Parliament's right to make laws. Since the mace was, originally, the weapon of the medieval clergy, the link between church and Parliament was signified as well. Through the years, the mace had also become a symbol of authority for universities and cities.

The original House of Commons mace was destroyed in the 1916 fire, but London's goldsmiths graciously remade it, using the silver and gold lumps that were found among the ashes of the original Centre Block. It is ceremonially carried into the House of Commons at the beginning of each sitting day, and, since 1995, has been left on display during the summer. Members of Parliament are not allowed

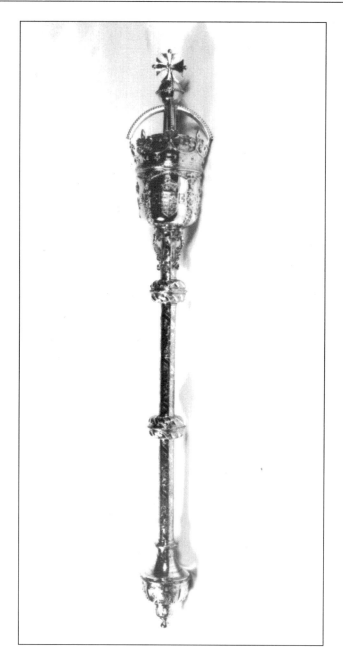

The mace, a symbol of power, must be present for the House of Commons to be in session.

(Photo: Andy Shott)

to try to interfere with the mace's removal at adjournment. Members who do so have to endure a reprimand at the Bar of the House of Commons or give up their seat.

The House of Commons functions through a combination of law, tradition, and private co-operation between political parties that work together to ensure the House can do its job. The way it operates protects both the right of the government to govern and the opposition parties to oppose.

A typical day in the House of Commons begins with private prayers. Most mornings are spent debating legislation, with, unless the issues are controversial, a token number of members of each party present. During many Commons debates, members engage each other in sometimes spirited question-and-answer discussions. While the House of Commons is considering bills, committees are at work in other parts of the Parliament Hill complex giving more detail scrutiny to legislation, hearing from witnesses, and dealing with potential amendments.

When bills are given first reading, they are not debated. Sometimes, although it is quite rare, they are referred to a committee after first reading, so that members of Parliament may help craft the legislation before it is actually debated by the full House of Commons.

At second reading, a bill's principles are debated, but not its specifics. If a bill passes this stage, it is sent to a committee for clause-by-clause consideration. The bill may be reported back by the committee, or, like most private members' bills, it may be left to die.

Bills that are sent back to the House of Commons by committees are then debated at "report stage." This is a crucial time in the passage of legislation. The fine details are discussed and amendments may be put forward. Once a bill passes report stage, it is usually given third reading after a short debate. Then it is sent to the Senate, which may make some amendments and send it back to the House of Commons. The Senate may also defeat the bill, unless it is a taxation law, or simply pass it. Once a bill passes, it is given Royal Assent. The bill becomes law when it is officially proclaimed and published in the Canada Gazette.

The House of Commons draws most of its public attention during the fifteen minutes that are set aside for short speeches by members, and the forty-five minute Question Period that follows it. The leader of the Opposition asks the first questions. Next, the official Opposition House Leader rises to pose a question, followed by the leader of the third party, and the House Leader for that party. After that, the rest of the members vie for the Speaker's attention. Opposition MPs usually ask the bulk of the questions, but near the end of Question Period, backbench government members are often allowed to pose questions to ministers.

Question Period is a uniquely Canadian creation. Since, in the United States, the president and Cabinet do not sit in the legislature, they can't be challenged for answers the way the Canadian prime minister and Cabinet can. In Britain, question time is severely limited.

Another Canadian innovation is the hour or so of media "scrums" that take place in the lobby of the House of Commons. Reporters wait for the prime minister, Cabinet ministers, and Opposition politicians to leave the chamber and face microphones. This is a time for politicians to be somewhat cautious, since they lose considerable protection against slander suits when they leave the House of Commons chamber. The crush of reporters can be intimidating to both members of the media and parliamentarians, but, unlike their counterparts in most other Western nations, Canadian journalists have easy access to politicians.

Following Question Period, members of Parliament may present petitions or raise points of order and questions of privilege. These are, essentially, complaints to the Speaker about actions inside the House of Commons or outside that might have improperly hampered a member of Parliament's work or have unfairly impinged on a member's honour.

In the few minutes after Question Period, ministers make statements about proposed legislation. Then the House of Commons continues its debate on legislation until the Motion to Adjourn is dealt with. This motion has little to do with the decision whether members of Parliament should leave or stay. Rather, it is a sort of miniature Question Period which allows members to pose longer questions to the government. Since few Cabinet ministers attend regularly, the debates are usually between backbench government and Opposition members.

Directly above the Speaker are two tiers of seats for members of the Parliamentary Press Gallery. There are far more journalists belonging to the press gallery than there are seats: more than 350 reporters, photographers, researchers, and technical support. Most watch the House of Commons on television or wait in the lobby to scrum members of Parliament when they leave. Only on special occasions, when an important dignitary addresses the House of Commons, is there a scramble for seats.

Above the press gallery are tiers of seats for the public. To the Speaker's left, at the same level as the lower tier of press gallery seats, are chairs for visiting members of the Senate and their guests. The prime minister has a set of seats directly opposite his chair, where important guests, friends, and members of the prime minister's family are seated. At the southern end of this gallery are seats for visiting diplomats.

Above the government benches are seats for political staff of all parties and for guests of Opposition MPs. The same is true for the lower tiers of seats directly opposite the Speaker, on the south side of the chamber. A translation booth is discreetly tucked in the southeast corner of the House of Commons chamber. Television cameras, controlled by the sergeant-at-arms, who, along with the clerk of the House, sits in front of the Speaker, peek out from the curtains that separate the House of Commons chamber from the members' lobbies that lie behind the government and Opposition benches. These are comfortable lounges where members can relax and talk outside the gaze of the public and press. Formerly, they were open to journalists.

The ceiling of the House of Commons is a single piece of painted Irish linen. Supporting it are gilded cherubs and heraldic symbols. Each of the stain glass windows of the House of Commons commemorates a province. Carvings of prehistoric animals symbolize our country's long natural history. The chairs and rugs of the House of Commons chambers are green, a symbolic reminder of the days when common people met to discuss their issues in public parks.

All attention in the House of Commons is centered on the Speaker, a member of Parliament who is elected by secret ballot to preside over the House of Commons. The Speaker is non-partisan. As well as being responsible for maintaining the House of Commons' rules and presiding over its debates, the Speaker is also in charge of the operation of the Parliament Hill complex. A lovely country house in the Gatineau Park, Kingsmere, which was bequeathed to Canada by William Lyon Mackenzie King, is the Speaker's home. The original Centre Block contained the Speaker's living quarters. These have been replaced with a complex of offices, a private dining room, and desks for the Speaker's staff. As the senior official of the House of

Looking down from the galleries of the House of Commons are
dozens of odd mythical creatures.

(Photo: Andy Shott)

Commons, the Speaker has a responsibility to welcome guests to our country's Parliament.

The Speaker is aided by a Deputy and several Assistant Deputy Speakers. The Speaker's chair can accommodate people of all sizes. Jeanne Sauvé, a former Speaker who later served as governor general, was a petite woman. A hydraulic lift system was installed in the Speaker's chair so Mme Sauvé could see and be seen.

The Speaker acts as the spokesperson of the House in its relations with the Crown, the Senate, and authorities outside Parliament. The holder of this office also acts to protect the rights of MPs and the dignity of Parliament. The Speaker is the chief executive of Parliament Hill.

The position of Speaker requires a considerable amount of study. Newcomers to the position can feel swamped by the massive amount of written law they must absorb, the age-old traditions that must be maintained, and the constant struggle by MPs to be heard. The Speaker must always be, and appear to be, impartial. The Speaker never participates in debate and must give serious consideration to any allegation that a member's rights have been infringed.

Even in the hottest debates, all speeches and questions must be addressed to the Speaker. The members must listen to and obey the Speaker's rulings, must wait for the Speaker to recognize them before they may speak, and are subject to the Speaker's discipline.

The strongest penalty the Speaker can impose upon a member is to "name" the MP, and the threat of naming is usually enough to ensure respect for the Speaker's authority. A member is named for disregarding the Speaker's authority when, for example, the member has refused a request to withdraw unparliamentary language, to desist in irrelevant or repetitious debate, or to stop interrupting a member who is addressing the House. Persisting in any other disorderly conduct when warned by the Speaker to desist is also a defiance of authority of the Chair which can lead to naming. The Speaker has two options: he or she may immediately order the offending member to withdraw from the chamber for the balance of the day's sitting. Alternatively, the Speaker may simply wait for the House to take whatever disciplinary action it deems appropriate. The first is an option introduced in February 1986. Should the Speaker choose the second alternative, however, another member — usually the Government House Leader — will immediately propose a motion to suspend the offending member. Such a motion is neither debatable nor amendable. Once the motion for suspension has been proposed, the Speaker will put the question. If the motion carries, the member must withdraw from the chamber and is also prevented from sitting in Committees of the Whole and in legislative, standing, or special committees for the duration of the suspension.

The Speaker relies on the clerk of the House for procedural advice, to help steer through the mass of law and precedent that guide the House of Commons. The clerk is also responsible for a wide range of tasks relating to the proceedings and official records of the House and its committees.

The clerk is assisted at the table in front of the Speaker by the deputy clerk, the clerk assistant (Procedural Services), the general legislative counsel, and several principal clerks and deputy principal clerks. These officials share duties at the table on a regular basis and may sit on the clerk's behalf in a temporary absence. The various procedural branches (Committees, Public Bills, Journals, Table Research and Private Members' Business) report to the clerk through the principal clerks.

THE SENATE

THERE ARE 104 SENATORS, appointed on a provincial and regional basis: Ontario and Quebec each have twenty-four; Nova Scotia and New Brunswick, ten respectively; six come from British Columbia, Alberta, Saskatchewan, Manitoba and Newfoundland; Prince Edward Island has four; there is one each for the Yukon and Northwest Territories.

The Senate, Canada's upper house, gives second consideration to all bills passed by the House of Commons.

(Photo: Andy Shott)

This regional representation is central to the role of the Senate in our system of government, and the chamber serves as a forum for the expression of regional concerns.

Apart from its traditional responsibility to reconsider legislation previously passed by the Commons, the Senate is involved in other, earlier, stages of the parliamentary process as well. Bills can be introduced there, and some of the closest scrutiny given to legislation from either House takes place in Senate committees, whose consideration of bills — often occurring while they are still being deliberated in the Commons — results in important improvements and amendments accepted by both chambers. In addition to their duties in the chamber itself and to intensive committee work, senators are engaged in governmental, parliamentary and even diplomatic activities. The Government Leader in Senate is normally a Cabinet member.

The Senate Chamber, sometimes called the Red Chamber, is built of limestone and panelled in Canadian oak. The paintings on both side walls depict scenes of World War I. The chamber measures twenty-six metres by thirteen metres. Proceedings are conducted in English and French, and a simultaneous translation system permits the senators, the public, journalists, and officials to follow in the language of their choice.

The throne in the centre of the dais is used by the queen or her representative in Canada, the governor general, on ceremonial occasions such as the Opening of Parliament. For such events, the Speaker's chair in front of the throne is removed. The small throne to the left is for the use of the queen's consort or the spouse of the governor general, as the case may be.

The Opening of Parliament, the Royal Assent to Bills and the Prorogation of Parliament take place in the Senate

Chamber. On these occasions, the Speaker and members of the House of Commons attend at the Bar of the Senate Chamber after being duly summoned to do so.

The Speaker of the Senate presides at sittings of the Senate, occupying the Speaker's chair in front of the throne. The Leader of the Government in the Senate sits on the side of the chamber to the right of the Speaker, and the leader of the Opposition sits on the side of the chamber to the left. The mace, the symbol of the authority of the Senate, rests on the clerk's table in the centre aisle when the Senate is in session. The news media, whose gallery is above the throne, report and comment on the proceedings in the chamber.

THE PEACE TOWER

ORIGINALLY, THE DESIGNERS of the new Centre Block wanted to call the high bell tower at its front entrance the "Victory Tower" as a tribute to Canada's role in World War I. The government decided, however, that it would commemorate the nation's desire for peace between the peoples of the world.

On the third floor of the Peace Tower is the Memorial Chamber, one of the most sacred places in Canada. It commemorates all those who gave their lives in Canada's wars and peacekeeping operations since Confederation. It is a small chapel that normally houses the Books of Remembrance, in which the names of all of Canada's war dead are recorded. A page is turned each day in a ceremony held at 11 A.M., to commemorate the hour of the armistice of 11 November 1918. Each name appears once each year. The constable stationed in the chamber will tell visitors on what day a certain name can be seen.

Each of the bells in the Peace Tower carillon is carefully tuned so
that the tower itself becomes a musical instrument.

(Photo: Andy Shott)

The Memorial Chapel in the Peace Tower is one of the country's most sacred places.

(National Archives of Canada C 10080)

The Memorial Chapel is a peaceful room of white marble and gentle light. Carvings commemorate the regiments that have fought for Canada. There is even sculpture to commemorate the animals who died in service to our country.

The beautiful ceiling, walls, and columns of the chamber are constructed of Château Gaillard stone presented by France. The altar is a gift of Great Britain, while the border and altar steps are fashioned from black marble, donated by the people of Belgium.

The chamber floor is made of stone quarried in the areas where Canadians fought. Brass plaques are made of shell casings and engraved with the names of the major battles of the First World War — Ypres, Mont Sorrel, the Somme, Vimy Ridge, Hill 70, Passchendaele, Amiens, Arras, Cambrai, Valenciennes and Mons — are inlaid in the floor.

Three stained-glass windows depict allegorical scenes entitled The Call to Arms (east window), The Assembly of Remembrance (south window) and The Dawn of Peace (west window). The walls are lined with seventeen panels recalling moments in Canada's military past.

While the Peace Tower was refurbished, the Books of Remembrance were placed below a sculpture in the Hall of Honour that commemorates the bravery and kindness of the military nurses who served Canada during the country's wars.

As a huge crowd gathered on the lawn of Parliament Hill to celebrate the fiftieth anniversary of Confederation, a sound rolled across the Ottawa Valley that had never been heard in Canada before. The newly built Peace Tower, which commemorates Canada's sacrifices in the nation's wars, had been transformed into a rare musical instrument — a carillon.

A carillon is an instrument that consists of at least twenty-three bells played from a keyboard. Each bell is tuned with great precision by paring metal away, usually from the bell's inside surface. Correctly tuned, the partials (component tones constituting the bell's sound) blend so harmoniously that many bells so tuned may be sounded together in a variety of chords.

The Peace Tower carillon consists of fifty-three bells. They were cast and tuned in the foundry of Gillett and Johnston in Croydon, England. The largest bell weighs 10,160 kilograms and sounds the note E. The smallest weighs only 4.5 kilograms and is pitched to the A, four and a half octaves higher. The art of carillon building was lost after the Renaissance, but has recently been rediscovered. The Peace Tower carillon is played from the type of large wooden keyboard that the Flemish invented three centuries ago.

The elevator that takes visitors to the Peace Tower observation deck actually moves on a skewed track so as to avoid the carillon. During recent Peace Tower renovations, the clock and carillon were stopped. The newly refurbished tower is, again, sending its beautiful tones across the capital.

THE HALL OF HONOUR

THE HALL OF HONOUR was completed in 1950, except for several of the commemorations. The hall links Confederation Hall to the main door of the Library of Parliament. Carvings represent the original Great Seal of Canada, with Queen Victoria enthroned. The war nurses are also commemorated, along with the people who died in the 1916 Centre Block fire and the Fathers of Confederation.

The Hall of Honour links Confederation hall and the Library of Parliament. Carvings commemorate Canadians who have served their country.

(Photo: Andy Shott)

The Hall of Honour is used for important state occasions, such as the lying-in state of former prime ministers, receptions of visiting dignitaries, and government banquets.

COMMITTEE ROOMS

TWO QUITE DIFFERENT committee rooms may be entered from the Hall of Honour. To the left, facing the library, is the Reading Room, which, until recently, was a newspaper and magazine library for members of Parliament. Commemorative paintings on the walls pay tribute to freedom of speech and a free press. At the Reading Room's entrance, the faces of famous journalists are

The House of Commons Reading Room was a place where members of Parliament and journalists scanned the country's daily and weekly newspapers. It now has smaller quarters on the first floor of the Centre Block, and this room is used for committee hearings.

(National Archives of Canada PA 39213)

commemorated in stone sculpture. A new, much smaller, reading room has been built one floor below to replace this room.

To the right, the Railway Committee Room has served since 1925 as a main meeting place for parliamentary committees. Both of these large rooms serve as the setting for important social functions held by the Government of Canada and members of Parliament.

THE SENATE FOYER

THE FAR EASTERN front doors of the Centre Block open to a flight of stairs that lead to the elegant foyer of the Senate. Red leather couches grace the halls. Above them are paintings of monarchs who have reigned over Canada: King George III and his wife, Queen Charlotte, to the right as the visitor faces the front doors of the Senate; the young Queen Victoria, the picture that has been rescued from two major fires; replicas of the portraits of King Edward VII, Queen Alexandra, King George V, and Queen Mary, all of which were lost in the 1916 blaze.

Above, carved in the stonework, are the faces of sculptors who worked on the building. They are supposed to be the faces of Vikings, but, of course, very few Vikings wore stone masons' goggles.

THE HOUSE OF COMMONS FOYER

THE HOUSE OF COMMONS foyer is somewhat smaller than the Senate foyer. It holds a small memorial to Lieut.-Col. G.H. Baker, a member of Parliament who was killed during World War I. Sculptures in the foyer were completed in

1975 by Eleanor Milne, the parliamentary stone mason. The ceiling of the foyer holds allegorical figures of trade and commerce. Stone carvings of Henry VII, founder of the Tudor dynasty, and George I, first king of the House of Hanover, watch over the door used by government members. The seals of the four provinces that were partners in Confederation in 1867 are set into the foyer's limestone walls.

THE PRIME MINISTER'S OFFICE

A STAIRWAY THAT begins on the left side of the House of Commons foyer leads to the prime minister's legislative office on the floor above. This elegant suite of offices is one of two prime minister's offices on Parliament Hill. The other is in the Langevin Block, across the street. Prime ministers' offices tend to wander, depending on the person holding the office. During the Trudeau and Mulroney years, this office was mainly used to greet important visitors and for dealing with House of Commons matters. Most executive business took place in the East Block during Trudeau's term, or in the Langevin Block during the Mulroney administration. The Centre Block suite became the main prime minister's office during the Chrétien years. Directly above the prime minister's office is the suite used by the leader of the Opposition.

Down the hall from the prime minister's office is the Cabinet room. Around an oval table, members of the Cabinet sit in red chairs, with the prime minister presiding in a high-backed, slightly larger chair. The room is fairly small, but elegantly furnished.

THE LIBRARY OF PARLIAMENT

At the end of the Hall of Honour is the Library of Parliament. This showpiece of Gothic revival architecture features an intricate parquet floor of cherry, oak, and walnut. In its panelling of Canadian white pine are carved hundreds of flowers, masks, and mythical creatures. Dominating the circular, domed room is a white marble statue of Queen Victoria which is so heavy that the pillar supporting it extends all the way to the bedrock below.

The library is a cornerstone of Parliament. Many MPs, senators and members of the press gallery would not be able to function without it. The library's elite staff of researchers and curators use computer technology to provide information, reference and research services to parliamentarians, political staff, and members of the media. It also serves the diplomatic community and visiting scholars.

The main library in the Centre Block represents only a fraction of the Library of Parliament's operations: most library employees, including all of the large Research Branch, are in other buildings, four of which house branch libraries and reading rooms.

The Library of Parliament originated in the legislative libraries of Upper and Lower Canada, created in the 1790s. These libraries were amalgamated when Upper and Lower Canada were united in 1841. As the new Province of Canada did not have a permanent capital for some time, the Legislature and its library moved from Kingston to Montreal and then alternated between Toronto and Quebec City for several years. Books were damaged and lost with each move.The collection has also been threatened by fire on three occasions. The most disastrous blaze was in Montreal in 1849, when a Loyalist mob protesting the Rebellion Losses Bill burned down the Legislature and destroyed all but two hundred of the twelve thousand books.

The library building, designed in the Gothic revival style by Thomas Fuller and Chilion Jones, opened in 1876. Its circular shape, galleries, and alcoves were the creation of Alpheus Todd, the chief librarian. He recommended that the building be "spacious and lofty" and wisely advised that it be separated from the Centre Block by a corridor to protect it from fire.

It survived the 1916 blaze, but in 1952, a fire broke out in the cupola of the library itself, causing extensive smoke and water damage. The library's wood panelling had to be dismantled, sent to Montreal for cleaning and partial fireproofing, and reinstalled. A replica of the intricate parquet floor was created in cherry, oak, and walnut.

THE "HOT ROOM"

THE PARLIAMENTARY PRESS GALLERY offices, on the Centre Block's third floor, resemble a small newsroom. The "Hot

The "Hot Room," the press headquarters of the Centre Block, looked tidy in the 1950s. Today, it's a jumble of desks and computers.
(National Archives of Canada PA 48151)

Room" is the headquarters for reporters from regional newspapers and radio stations, freelancers, and some staff of Canadian Press. Formerly, it housed the entire press gallery. Now, however, with more than 350 members, the press gallery has been split. Larger bureaus use space in the National Press Building, across the street from the West Block, or rent office space in buildings along Sparks Street.

BEHIND CLOSED DOORS

THE CENTRE BLOCK remains a fairly self-sufficient home for members of Parliament, but gone are the days when it was a warren of small apartments, with living space for many of its senior officials. There are still a few private places that are off-limits to the public. The Speakers of the Senate and the House of Commons have spacious offices, libraries, and entertainment rooms, which are used often as reception places for visiting dignitaries. Senators have a small reading room, furnished with comfortable red-leather sofas and chairs. The Parliamentary Restaurant offers fine dining to parliamentarians, senior staff members, and journalists. People taking tours of the Centre Block see most of the more impressive parts of the building. Even though it is the centre of the Canadian legislative process, it is still, essentially, an office building, with most of its space being used by members of Parliament and senators as their administrative headquarters.

Part Four
The Hill

THE EAST AND WEST BLOCKS

HE EAST AND West Blocks were supposed to be constructed "in a plain, substantial style of architecture, of coarse, hammer-dressed masonry." No one would describe the East and West Blocks of today's Parliament Buildings as "plain." In fact, the architecture is so elaborate and ornate that it doesn't even have a name. Usually, the two buildings are described as "Victorian," or "Gothic," but those terms don't come close to expressing the multitude of bizarre styles that were incorporated in their design.

The departmental buildings, as they were called at the time of Confederation, arose amid scandal. Part of the problem was the government's incompetence when it came to issuing tenders and instructions. The government wanted the buildings erected quickly and at a ridiculously low price. Looking back, it's easy to see how honest builders would have stayed away from the project while contractors who were willing to be late and go over budget were prepared to take on the work. The government wanted the East and West Blocks built for $278,810. While the buildings were

The Mackenzie Tower rises above the West Block of the Parliament Buildings.

(Photo: Mark Bourrie)

somewhat smaller than they are now (some towers were added later, and both buildings were expanded after Confederation), the price was almost as ridiculous then as it is today.

No test borings were done on the hill's shattered bedrock. No ventilation or heating system was planned for either building. Work began even before the designs were finished. The same strikes that caused problems on the Centre Block project hit the departmental buildings. Investigations and political scandals stopped the work. The deadline for the buildings' completion, 1 February 1862 was a sad day: the edifices were empty of workers, the money had run out, and the construction site looked more like a snow-covered ruin than a future capitol.

The East Block still looks much the same as it did before Confederation.

(Photo: Mark Bourrie)

Of course, the two buildings were eventually completed, despite the financial scandals that surrounded their construction. Over the years, they have been renovated, received additions, and even survived small fires.

Of the two old buildings, the West Block has undergone the most change. Externally, it is still, one might argue, the most impressive building on the hill, especially when seen from Bank Street or the road that leads down to the river walkway and lower parking area. Inside, it has been badly abused. It was damaged by fire in 1899; then, in the fit of "modernization" that struck governments in the middle of the century, it was gutted. All its original rooms disappeared.

Fortunately, the East Block hasn't suffered the same fate. It remains a functioning office building for senior ministers and members of Parliament, while housing offices that have been restored to appear the way they did in the years that followed Confederation. The restoration of the former offices of the governor general, Sir John A. Macdonald, Sir Georges Etienne Cartier, and the old Cabinet office simply required redecorating the old offices and the gathering together of the original furniture. The occupants of those offices, which, over the years, had been converted for the use of the prime minister and the minister of external affairs, had respected their heritage. Sir John A. Macdonald's old desk simply had to be wheeled down the hall, since it was still in use in the East Block in the late 1970s.

If any building on Parliament Hill has ghosts, it's the East Block. Every prime minister from Macdonald to Trudeau has had his office on the building's second floor, on the side that faces the main lawn of Parliament Hill. While prime ministers also had offices in the Centre Block and in the Langevin Block (and Mackenzie King worked out of the bizarre attic library that can still be seen at Laurier House in

Sandy Hill), the East Block prime minister's office was the place where many of the nation's secrets were kept. The East Block is a place that has never seemed particularly welcome to visitors. In fact, the restored rooms on the second floor are among the least appreciated of the capital's political shrines. In the past, when the East Block was home to the entire Cabinet, to the prime minister and the governor general (who spent his work days just down the hall from the prime minister), while it also held the nation's gold reserves in its basement vaults, tourists were not admitted.

Since the renovations, after years of being bricked up, the old governor general's entrance has been reopened. A

The governor general's entrance of the East Block portrays the royal coat of arms. It was reopened after recent renovations.

(Photo: Mark Bourrie)

chamber of meditation is dedicated to former member of Parliament Sean Sullivan, who left a promising political career to become a Roman Catholic priest. Father Sullivan's time as a priest was tragically cut short by cancer.

The West Block is closed to the public, and will be until the cafeteria has been rebuilt to hold the House of Commons during the interior renovations to the Centre Block. The East Block is one of Canada's overlooked national treasures. In the summer and on weekends during the rest of the year, tours take people through the old, restored offices while guides recount the lore of this building which was so central to Canada's government during the formative years of the nation.

THE FUTURE OF PARLIAMENT HILL

LIKE THE COUNTRY itself, the parliamentary precincts are in a process of continual renewal. The end of the twentieth century finds Parliament Hill in the midst of the largest construction project since the completion of the new Centre Block.

The cost of the work may run as high as $500 million. Small earthquakes, acid rain, and normal wear and tear have left much of the masonry on all the buildings in a state of bad repair. In some places, most of the mortar between the stonework has dissolved. On the Centre Block, more than forty-eight kilometres of mortar joints are being replaced. Many of the carvings need to be restored and cleaned. The copper roof on the Centre Block has been replaced. The new copper sheeting should last another century.

Part of the Centre Block's problem was the choice of stone. The sandstone blocks on the exterior of the building

This ornate doorway on the West Block bears the coat of arms of the Province of Canada.

(Photo: Mark Bourrie)

suck up salt water from the streets. Incredibly, the salts are drawn into the entire stone facade and can only be removed through the application of a special poultice to the stones. The Peace Tower acts as a giant ventilation chimney pulling moist air into the exterior stonework.

Inside, the plumbing needs to be brought up to date. So do the electrical system, ventilation, telephone linkages, and television cable. Insulation needs to be removed.

In 2002, the House of Commons will move into temporary quarters in the West Block. During the next four years, the Commons chamber will be restored. Then, in

The West Block of the Parliament Buildings house offices for members of Parliament and the Cabinet. During renovations to the Centre Block, it will be home to the House of Commons and the Senate.

(Photo: Mark Bourrie)

2006, the Senate will move into the same West Block hall to allow its present home to go through a four-year-long renewal.

The exteriors of the West Block, Confederation Building, and the Department of Justice buildings will also be restored, while their plumbing, electrical, and communications systems are upgraded. Asbestos insulation, a potential hazard to workers in the Parliament Hill complex, will be removed.

LIFE ON THE HILL

PARLIAMENT HILL HAS become a gathering place for Canadians, especially during the summer tourist season. While parliamentarians are on summer recess, thousands of visitors tour the Centre Block and the East Block and enjoy the spectacular vistas from lookouts along the cliff.

At midnight of 1 July 1967, the Centennial Flame was lit on Parliament Hill.

(National Archives of Canada PA 11375)

The Centennial Flame celebrates the unity of Canada.
(Photo: Mark Bourrie)

One of the Hill's most famous landmarks is the Centennial Flame. It was lit at midnight, 1 January 1967, by Prime Minister Lester B. Pearson to mark the end of Canada's first hundred years as a country and the beginning of its second century. The light from the Centennial Flame, which glows among the shields of the provinces and territories, is supposed to show the way as Canada moves toward its bicentennial. The water that flows from the base of the flame and embraces all the provincial coats of arms, symbolises the nation's unity. The flame is a popular spot for tourists. Coins that are tossed into the fountain are distributed among local charities.

Sir John A. Macdonald still watches over Parliament Hill, which was his domain for a quarter of a century.

(Photo: Mark Bourrie)

The Hill has commemorations to many of Canada's prime ministers, and to the colonial leaders who guided Canada to independence and Confederation. Two of our monarchs, Queen Victoria and Queen Elizabeth II, are honoured as well. There are also small, rather eccentric, little places on the Hill that are missed by visitors. For example, halfway down the hill, between the East Block and the canal, visitors can still see parts of the "Lovers Walk" that used to run along the entire length of Parliament Hill. It was a private place where people could go to get away from the stress of their offices and the noise of the city.

On the edge of the hill, directly behind the statue of George Brown, a Father of Confederation, there is another oddity. The Rock of Gibraltar may have its apes, the Tower

Lester Pearson won the Nobel Peace Prize before serving as prime minister from 1963 until 1968.

(Photo: Mark Bourrie)

The statue of Prime Minister John Diefenbaker keeps watch over Parliament Hill.

(Photo: Mark Bourrie)

of London its ravens, but on Canada's Parliament Hill, the roost is ruled by cats. There are big, powerful tabbies, graceful Persians, tortoise-shell cats, and cats that look like patchwork quilts.

They have been there longer than the politicians; they arrived before construction of the Parliament Buildings began. The little colony has lasted through wars, depressions, and the loss of the original Centre Block. Cat-hating administrators have never been able to get rid of them. After more than a century of fending for themselves, the felines of the Hill have got it made. Now they enjoy free food and veterinary care, thanks to donations of time and money by cat lovers.

René Chartrand, who is spending his retirement years looking after the animals, has guaranteed that the half-wild creatures won't starve or be driven from Parliament Hill by bureaucrats who feel they don't belong there. Chartrand worked at many different jobs before he retired. He was a house painter, a labourer in the local paper mills, and a factory foreman. Since he took up the cats' cause, he has become a familiar face to prime ministers, Cabinet members and the hundreds of people who visit the animals every day.

A small temporary stable used by the RCMP in the summer months is just to the west of the West Block. On the West Block itself, on the corner closest to the Centennial Flame, is a small door which was used by Prime Minister Mackenzie when he wanted to slip past people looking for government jobs. It was last used by Prime Minister Trudeau to avoid reporters when he left his office to call an election in 1968.

Behind the Centre Block is the bell that crashed down from the clock tower of the Centre Block at the height of the Fire of 1916. Nearby is a statue of D'Arcy McGee, the only

D'Arcy McGee, Irish rebel and Father of Confederation who was assassinated on Sparks Street in 1868, is commemorated in a statue that has had adventures of its own.

(National Archives of Canada PA 34427)

federal Cabinet minister to be assassinated in Canadian history. He was killed by a Fenian assailant at a boarding house on Sparks Street, between Metcalfe and O'Connor. Like McGee, who was once sentenced to death *in absentia* for taking part in a rebellion in Ireland, the statue has had its adventures. It was cast in Belgium in the summer of 1914. When German troops crossed the Belgian frontier, the statue was quickly buried. It survived the war unharmed, but, had it been found, it would probably have been melted down to make shell casings. Like so many other features of Parliament Hill, the McGee statue has its own interesting story to tell.

Appendix
The Prime Ministers of Canada

SIR JOHN ALEXANDER MACDONALD
1 July 1867 — 5 November 1873
17 October 1878 — 6 June 1891

Sir John Alexander Macdonald was born in Glasgow, Scotland, on 11 January 1815 and moved to Canada as a child. He articled with a Kingston law firm and practised law in that city until he was elected to the Parliament of the Province of Canada in 1844 at the age of twenty-nine. Two years later, he became a member of the Cabinet and served as joint-premier and in senior ministerial positions until Confederation. He was a major architect of the union of Canada, New Brunswick, and Nova Scotia in 1867, and became Canada's first prime minister. He was knighted for his success in bringing about an agreement between the three colonial governments. Macdonald also succeeded in bringing the Hudson's Bay Company's huge Rupert's Land territory under Canadian control, negotiated the entry of British Columbia and Prince Edward Island into the Canadian federation, and helped establish the province of Manitoba. Except for the term of Alexander MacKenzie's Liberal government (1873 to 1878), Macdonald served as prime minister until his death in 1891. He lived at Earnscliff, on Sussex Drive, which is now the home of the British High Commissioner. Macdonald is buried in Kingston. The original prime minister's office in the East Block has been restored to look as it did late in his administration, in 1886.

ALEXANDER MACKENZIE
7 November 1873 — 9 October 1878

Alexander Mackenzie was born in Dunkeld, Scotland, in January 1821. As a young man, the future prime minister worked as a stonemason, building some of the fortifications in Kingston harbour; he even bid on the construction of the Parliament Buildings. In 1872, MacKenzie was elected to the House of Commons; he became prime minister when Macdonald's government fell in 1873. His government established the Supreme Court of Canada, the Royal Military College at Kingston, and the first secret ballot. He turned down a knighthood. After serving as prime minister, he remained a member of Parliament until he died in April 1892, less than a year after Macdonald.

SIR JOHN JOSEPH CALDWELL ABBOTT
16 June 1891 — 24 November 1892

John Abbott was the first senator to hold the office of prime minister. He took over the post on Macdonald's death, being sworn in on 16 June 1891. He resigned eighteen months later.

SIR JOHN SPARROW THOMPSON
5 December 1892 — 12 December 1894

Thompson took over from the caretaker administration of Abbott. A Halifax native, he was only forty-eight years old when he was asked to form a government. Thompson had already served as a distinguished member of Nova Scotia's Supreme Court and was one of the country's best lawyers. He died suddenly in London in December 1894, aged fifty, while visiting Queen Victoria at Windsor Castle. He was buried in Halifax.

Sir Mackenzie Bowell
21 December 1894 — 27 April 1896

This colourful politician served as prime minister for just over a year. He was essentially a caretaker leader, holding office until the Conservatives could choose someone to take them into the next election. He resigned in April 1896 but remained a senator for another twenty-three years. He died at the age of ninety-four.

SIR CHARLES TUPPER
1 May 1896 — 8 July 1896

Tupper was one month short of his seventy-fifth birthday when he became prime minister — the last one to serve out the term of Sir John A. Macdonald. He was a doctor and former premier of Nova Scotia. His tenure was shorter than that of any other prime minister. In a way, he deserved better, having been one of the key negotiators of Confederation.

SIR WILFRID LAURIER
11 July 1896 — 6 October 1911

Sir Wilfrid Laurier was born in the village of St. Lin, Quebec, in 1841. At the age of eleven, his father sent him to the village of New Glasgow to learn English. After his stay in New Glasgow, he studied classics and French literature for seven years at L'Assomption college. Laurier moved to Montreal, worked in a law office by day and studied law at night. This work prepared him for a career in politics, a field that suited him well because he had the ability to achieve consensus between the many factions in government. When he lost his position as prime minister in a controversial election on the Free Trade issue, he stayed on to play an important role in Opposition. Laurier's home in Sandy Hill, which he originally left to his successor and protégé, William Lyon Mackenzie King, is now a museum.

SIR ROBERT LAIRD BORDEN
10 October 1911 — 10 July 1920

Sir Robert Laird Borden was born at Grand Pré, Nova Scotia, in 1854. He became prime minister at the age of fifty-eight and led Canada through World War I. Borden's regime was extremely effective. It succeeded in mobilizing a divided nation and creating an enormous munitions industry. More than 280,000 Canadians volunteered to fight in France out of a nation of 8 million. The Great War cost Canada 60,000 lives, but the country emerged as a much more independent nation. Borden resigned in 1920, citing poor health. He died in 1937.

SIR ARTHUR MEIGHEN
10 July 1920 — 29 December 1921
29 June 1926 — 25 September 1926

Arthur Meighen was born in 1874 near Anderson, Ontario. He practised law in Manitoba as a young man and was elected to Parliament in 1908. After the resignation of Borden, he assumed the leadership of the Conservative Party but lost the subsequent election to Mackenzie King. He served one more brief term as prime minister, heading a minority government in 1926. His most valuable political role, however, was in Opposition during the King administration. After long service to the country, he died in Toronto in 1960.

WILLIAM LYON MACKENZIE KING
29 December 1921 — 28 June 1926
25 September 1926 — 7 August 1930
23 October 1935 — 15 November 1948

King was one of the country's most enigmatic politicians and certainly among the more interesting leaders in our history. Born in Kitchener, Ontario, in 1874, King was the grandson of firebrand revolutionary William Lyon Mackenzie. Their personalities, however, couldn't have been more dissimilar, although, in ideology, they had much in common. King attended the University of Toronto, where he shone as a scholar. A methodical man with a sharp mind, he went on to postgraduate studies at Chicago and Harvard. King guided Canada through much of the Great Depression, through World War II as well as the formative postwar years. After his resignation he retired to his estate at Kingsmere, in Gatineau Park. He died on 22 July 1950. King left his house in Sandy Hill and his estate at Kingsmere to Canada. Both are sites of museums dedicated to Canada's longest-serving chief executive.

Richard Bedford Bennett
7 August 1930 — 23 October 1935

No politician ever took over the reigns of office at a worse time than did R.B. Bennett. He came to power just as the Great Depression was tightening its grip on the country. Although he provoked public anger and jealousy because he was the richest prime minister and the only millionaire to hold office before Pierre Trudeau, Bennett's actions and correspondence show that he desperately wanted to pull the country out of its economic slump. He moved to England in 1938 and died there on 26 June 1947 after serving as a viscount in the House of Lords.

LOUIS STEPHEN ST. LAURENT
15 November 1948 — 21 June 1957

L ouis St. Laurent came to Ottawa after a career as one of the country's best corporate lawyers. He served as Prime Minister King's minister of justice and replaced King as Liberal party leader in November 1948. After six months in office, he called an election and won the biggest majority in Canadian history up to that time: 194 seats for the Liberals to 41 for the Conservatives. In the spring of 1957, the Progressive Conservatives formed a minority government. He stepped aside with dignity and, seven months later, gave up the Liberal leadership. He died in 1973.

JOHN GEORGE DIEFENBAKER
21 June 1957 — 22 April 1963

B orn in the hamlet of Neustadt, Ontario, sixty kilometres south
of Owen Sound, Diefenbaker spent his formative years in
Saskatchewan. Diefenbaker was a skilled criminal lawyer who
took on some of the toughest cases of his time. He won a
minority government in 1957 and, the next year, went on to form
a majority government with 208 of the 265 Commons seats. The
Diefenbaker regime was a stormy period in Canada's history as
the country struggled to define its place in the Cold War world.
After his defeat in 1963, he served as a colourful member of the
Opposition. When he died in 1980, he was mourned by political
friend and foe alike. He is buried at the Diefenbaker Centre at the
University of Saskatchewan in Saskatoon.

LESTER BOWLES PEARSON
22 April 1963 — 20 April 1968

Born on 23 April 1897 in the village of Newtonbrook, Ontario, Pearson attended the Universities of Toronto and Oxford. In 1948 St. Laurent appointed him external affairs minister. He was chairman of the council of NATO, president of the United Nations General Assembly and was proposed twice for the position of secretary-general of the United Nations, only to be vetoed by the Soviet Union on both occasions. Pearson was awarded the Nobel Peace Prize for his achievement at Suez and, during his administration, placed great emphasis on foreign affairs and on the renewal of federalism. After five years as prime minister, he retired. Pearson died of cancer on 27 December 1972 and was buried in a small cemetery overlooking the Gatineau Hills, at Wakefield, Quebec.

PIERRE ELLIOTT TRUDEAU
20 April 1968 — 3 June 1979
3 March 1980 — 30 June 1984

Trudeau, a lawyer, author, and political theorist, was born in Montreal on 18 October 1919. His first election victory won him a majority of 154 seats to 72 for the Conservatives, 23 for the NDP, and 14 Créditistes. Trudeau entered politics because he believed that Quebec would remain part of a strong Canadian federation if there was equality of opportunity for all Canadians. Much of his time in office was devoted to patriation of the Constitution, to entrenching a Charter of Rights, and strengthening the role of the federal government.

CHARLES JOSEPH CLARK
4 June 1979 — 3 March 1980

Clark was born and raised in High River, Alberta, and became Canada's youngest prime minister, taking office just before his fortieth birthday. His administration lasted less than a year. Clark later served as external affairs minister and was given responsibility for constitutional negotiations during the Mulroney administration.

JOHN NAPIER TURNER
30 June 1984 — 17 September 1984

Turner was born in Surrey, England, in 1929. He entered the first Trudeau Cabinet as minister of justice, later serving as finance minister. He left politics in 1975 to work as a corporate lawyer. In 1984, he won the Liberal leadership but lost the subsequent election. He stayed on as Liberal leader to fight the 1988 election.

MARTIN BRIAN MULRONEY
17 September 1984 — 24 June 1993

Mulroney was born at Baie-Comeau, Quebec, in 1939. After working as a Montreal-based corporate lawyer, Mulroney won the Conservative leadership in 1982. In the election held 4 September 1984, Mulroney won the largest federal majority in Canadian history. He negotiated the Free Trade Agreement with the United States and laid the groundwork for the North American Free Trade Agreement.

AVRIL PHAEDRA (KIM) CAMPBELL
25 June 1993 — 4 November 1993

Campbell's first elected office was as a member of the Vancouver Public School Board. She then worked as executive assistant to British Columbia premier William Bennett. After being elected as a Social Credit MLA, she ran for the Socred leadership herself, losing to Bill Vander Zalm in 1986. In 1988, she was elected to Parliament and served as justice minister and minister of national defence in the Mulroney government. In June 1993, she was elected leader of the Progressive Conservative Party of Canada and replaced Brian Mulroney as prime minister on 25 June 1993. She lost the general election that followed. In 1996, she was appointed to a diplomatic post in the United States.

JOSEPH-JACQUES-JEAN CHRÉTIEN
November 1993 —

Jean Chrétien was born in 1934 in Shawinigan, Quebec. He studied law at Laval University and came to Ottawa as one of the strong Quebec federalists who were drawn to national politics during the Pearson administration. He has held a variety of Cabinet portfolios, including Indian Affairs and Northern Development, Finance, and Justice. Chrétien was instrumental in the repatriation of the Canadian Constitution in 1982.

Bibliography

Beauchesne, Arthur, *Canada's Parliament Buildings*. Ottawa: King's Printer, 1948.

Dempson, Peter, *Assignment Ottawa*. Toronto: General Publishing Ltd., 1968.

Eggleson, W., *The Queen's Choice*. Ottawa: The National Capital Commission, 1961.

Laundy, Philip, *Canada's Parliament*. Ottawa: House of Commons, 1987.

Bearskin rugs, heavy wooden furniture, and a great fireplace gave a rustic air to the Speaker's Library that befitted the headquarters of an official of a great northern nation.

(National Archives of Canada C 3353)

The author's favourite stone carving on Parliament Hill is this forlorn moose, which watches over the Senate Speaker's entrance in the Centre Block.

(Photo: Mark Bourrie)

MacRae, Marion, *MacNab of Dundurn*. Toronto: Clarke Irwin, 1971.

Philips, R.A.J., *The East Block of the Parliament Buildings of Canada*. Ottawa: Queen's Printer, 1967.

White, Randall, *Ontario 1610-1985*. Toronto: Dundurn Press, 1985.

Varkaris, Jane, and Lucile Finsten, *Fire On Parliament Hill*. Erin: Boston Mills Press, 1988.